Daddy's Heroes®
Unforgettable Sports Moments To Share With Children

THE '86 METS, BUCKNER & THE BAMBINO

Tom Garcia and Karun Naga

Illustrated by Jenifer J. Donnelly

ISBN 978-0-9792111-1-9

It was a chilly October evening in New York City.

Lots of boys and girls and moms and dads arrived at Shea Stadium to watch the **New York Mets** play the **Boston Red Sox** in Game 6 of the 1986 World Series.

If the Red Sox could win, they would be the baseball champions.

Shea Stadium was the most exciting place to be in New York that night.

The Red Sox had not won the World Series for many, many years.

A long time ago, the Red Sox had the best baseball player of all time – *the Bambino*.

The Bambino could hit and the Bambino could throw. . . **the Bambino was the superhero of his time!**

With the Bambino, the Red Sox were winners.

But then, the
Red Sox traded the
Bambino to another
team and they
stopped winning.

Some people thought the Red Sox were haunted by the Bambino and the Bambino's spirit would never let the Red Sox win the World Series again.

This legend became known as…
THE CURSE OF THE BAMBINO.

The boys and girls rooting for the Mets were hoping that *The Curse of the Bambino* would strike again.

The big game started with **Rocket Roger** taking the mound for the Red Sox.

Rocket was one of the strongest pitchers in all of baseball, and he won lots of games for the Red Sox that year.

With Rocket on their side, the confident Red Sox took an early 2-0 lead.

There were hits, errors, and big plays throughout the night. Clutch hitters for the Mets, like **Ray Knight** and ***Gary "The Kid" Carter***, kept the Mets in the game. After nine innings of baseball, the score was tied 3-3.

The game went into the 10th inning to find a winner.

The Red Sox were up to bat first and quickly took a 5-3 lead thanks to a homerun from their heavy-hitting centerfielder, *Big Hendu*.

When the Mets got up to bat, it was the bottom of the 10th inning. Before they knew it, there were two outs and the Mets were still losing by two runs.

Just one more out and the Mets would lose!

Some Mets players were so sure they were about to lose, that they went to the clubhouse and got ready to go home.

But, were they giving up too soon???

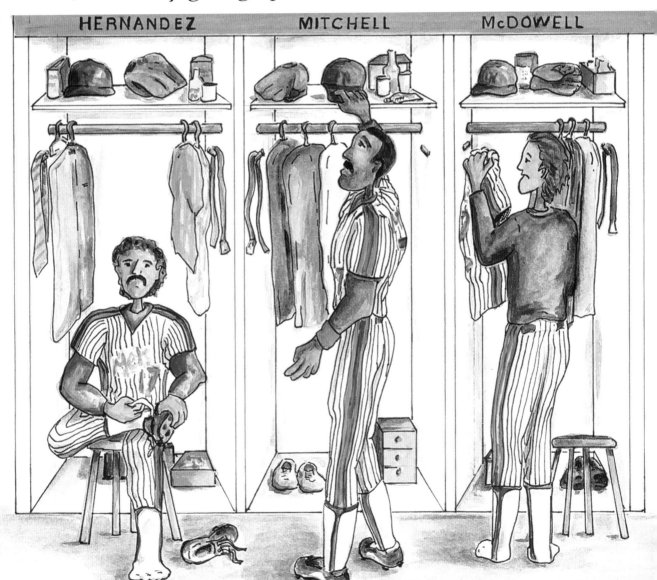

The boys and girls rooting for the Mets were hoping for a miracle.

Would the Bambino and his curse strike again???

And then. . .

. . . sure enough, with two outs in the bottom of the 10th inning, the scrappy Mets showed they weren't ready to give up!

First, Gary Carter got a hit.

Next, **Kevin Mitchell**, who was in the clubhouse just minutes before, got a hit.

And then, Ray Knight got a hit that brought Gary home to score.

The Mets only needed one run to tie the game!!!

By the time **Mookie Wilson** came to bat for the Mets, the boys and girls were screaming wildly and believed their Mets could win the game.

But, the Red Sox quickly got two strikes on Mookie.

The Mets were now only one strike from losing the game and the World Series.

With Kevin Mitchell on third, Mookie battled the Red Sox pitcher as both Red Sox and Mets fans grew nervous.

Somehow Mookie was able to fight off pitch after pitch.

One pitch was wild and Mookie jumped out of the way. The ball went past the catcher, and Kevin ran home to tie the score for the Mets!

The Bambino was lurking...

After fighting off five tough pitches, Mookie finally hit a slow ground ball towards first base.

Everyone thought that Bill Buckner, the Red Sox fielder, would make the easy play.

But the ball went right through Buckner's legs and Mookie was safe at first base!!!

When the ball rolled through Buckner's legs, Ray Knight was able to score the winning run for the Mets!

As Ray ran to home plate, the Mets and their fans celebrated as the Mets won Game 6.

What a comeback!

Maybe it was Mookie's speed that made Buckner miss the ball, but...maybe it was
The Curse of the Bambino...